Best Easy Day Hikes
West Los Angeles

Help Us Keep This Guide Up to Date

Every effort has been made by the author and editors to make this guide as accurate and useful as possible. However, many things can change after a guide is published—trails are rerouted, regulations change, facilities come under new management, etc.

We would appreciate hearing from you concerning your experiences with this guide and how you feel it could be improved and kept up to date. While we may not be able to respond to all comments and suggestions, we'll take them to heart and we'll also make certain to share them with the author. Please send your comments and suggestions to the following address:

> GPP
> Reader Response/Editorial Department
> P.O. Box 480
> Guilford, CT 06437

Or you may e-mail us at:

> editorial@GlobePequot.com

Thanks for your input, and happy trails!

Best Easy Day Hikes Series

Best Easy Day Hikes
West Los Angeles

Bryn Fox

FALCONGUIDES

GUILFORD, CONNECTICUT
HELENA, MONTANA

AN IMPRINT OF GLOBE PEQUOT PRESS

FALCONGUIDES®

TOPO! Explorer software and SuperQuad source maps courtesy of National Geographic Maps. For information about TOPO! Explorer, TOPO!, and Nat Geo Maps products, go to www.topo.com or www.natgeomaps.com.

Maps created by Designmaps Inc. © Morris Book Publishing, LLC

Library of Congress Cataloging-in-Publication Data is available on file.

ISBN 978-0-7627-5260-7

Printed in the United States of America

10 9 8 7 6 5 4 3 2 1

Contents

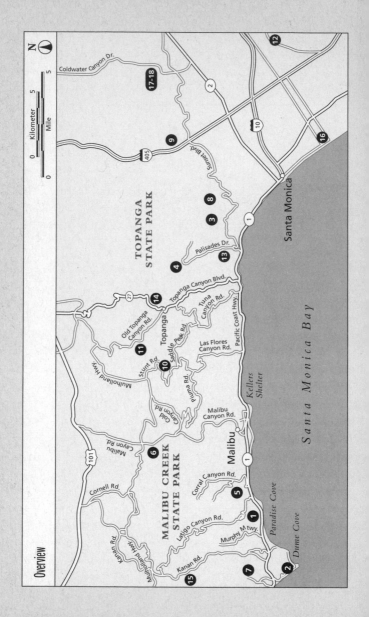

Overview

N

Kilometer 5

Mile 5

Coldwater Canyon Dr.

TOPANGA STATE PARK

MALIBU CREEK STATE PARK

Santa Monica Bay

Santa Monica

Malibu

Palisades Dr.

Topanga Canyon Blvd.

Old Topanga Canyon Rd.

Mulholland Hwy.

Stunt Rd.

Saddle Peak Rd.

Piuma Rd.

Old Canyon Rd.

Malibu Canyon Rd.

Tuna Canyon Rd.

Las Flores Canyon Rd.

Pacific Coast Hwy.

Keller's Shelter

Coral Canyon Rd.

Latigo Canyon Rd.

Cornell Rd.

Kanan Rd.

Murphy M twy.

Mulholland Hwy.

Kanan Rd.

Sunset Blvd.

Paradise Cove

Dunne Cove

Topanga

Acknowledgments

Many thanks go out to all of my friends and hiking buddies who made every sweaty mile come with an extra laugh. Thanks to Jenny, who wins the award for not dumping me as a friend after the hottest hike ever; Josephine, who wins for best ability to humorously bond with the wildlife; and Jannine, who wins for her innate ability to keep two outdoor-crazy dogs out of trouble and untangled. And most of all, enormous thanks to my husband, Ben, who hiked both the fun and the not-so-fun days with me, and went way above and beyond his husbandly duties to help me finish this book, despite a surprisingly crazy time in my life.

Introduction

When I was a student at UCLA, people were often surprised to hear that I was an outdoor instructor. "There aren't any 'outdoors' in LA" was often the response I received. But I was pleased to rebut that LA is brimming with outdoor adventures to be had—you simply had to know where to look. The Santa Monica Mountains run east to west, stretching all the way from Will Rogers Park to Point Mugu, and provide literally hundreds of miles of trails to hike. Within the Santa Monica Mountains is a variety of state parks including Will Rogers State Park, Malibu Creek State Park, and Zuma/Trancas Canyon, all of which have hiking trails and often offer facilities such as picnic tables and restrooms. Any of these areas can be easily reached from Santa Monica and provide a wide variety of hiking options from easy strolls that can be done in an hour to more enduring challenges that will take all day. But whatever your hiking desires, there is a vast and beautiful landscape awaiting your hiking shoes in the mountains of West LA.

Weather

The beauty of hiking in Southern California is that it can be done literally any month of the year. Los Angeles has a very mild climate with temperatures ranging from highs in the upper 60s in the winter to highs in the upper 80s in the summer, making for relatively pleasant hiking temperatures all year. One thing to note, however, is that West LA covers a large region, from the beaches of Malibu to the inland areas of Topanga Canyon, and temperatures can be cool

1

and comfortable at the beach while being much hotter a few miles inland. It is a good idea to stick to trails closer to the coast on the hottest days of summer and save the inland hikes for cooler days. On the other hand, some of the inland waterfall hikes can be beautiful on dreary days just after a rain as the falls are likely to be pumping. Rainfall peaks during January and February and becomes almost nonexistent during the summer months.

Wilderness Restrictions/Regulations

The hikes in this book fall under the discretion of various governing agencies, depending on where you are. Many of the trails in this book are within state park boundaries. The state parks included are Will Rogers State Park, Malibu Creek State Park, and Topanga State Park. Other hikes are on National Park Service land while others still are governed by the Mountains Restoration Trust, Santa Monica Mountains Conservancy, or city parks. Each governing agency has its own set of laws and rules so it is important not to skip over the "fees and permits" section of each chapter or the laws about dogs, as these tend to vary from one agency to the next.

On National Park Service land there is usually no fee to park or use the trails, but you will need a permit to camp overnight. There are also no official operating hours, meaning you can hike the trails at any time. Dogs are usually allowed on National Park Service land as long as they are kept on a leash.

In state parks the rules are different. Most state parks require a parking fee. Make sure you have cash on hand as there are often just deposit boxes with no one available to offer change. State parks have specific hours and are usually open sunrise to sunset. Dogs are not allowed in Topanga State Park or Malibu Creek State Park, though leashed dogs are permitted in Will Rogers State Park.

Any hikes not on state park or National Park Service land have their own set of rules. Be sure to check the hike specs for specific information.

Safety

Hiking through West LA can involve anything from an urban walk on a paved park path to a challenging hike up a steep slope. Because of the variety of types of hikes you will find in this book, the level of precaution you must take will vary greatly as well. There's no need to fear the elements when hiking to the Baldwin Hills Overlook; however, while hiking through the Santa Monica Mountains you will want to take some extra precautions to avoid hazards like mountain lions and poison oak.

Fires

Forest fires have ravaged the city of Malibu and its surrounding area probably more times than you can recall watching the resident celebrities evacuating on the news. The surrounding hillsides well up into the crest of the mountain range have also burned in a number of historic fires. It is important to note that because of the great fire danger in this dry climate, fires are prohibited anywhere on park service land, except for in specific campsites. Each campsite has its own set of rules so if you are interested in a weenie roast, be sure to ask if fires are permitted, and build fires *only* in designated fire rings.

Wildlife

Though it is unlikely you will encounter any dangerous wildlife on your trip (you may not see more than some small lizards when hiking in this area), you are likely to find bees and ticks, and even mountain lions and rattlesnakes on occasion.

- Mountain lions are seen in the Santa Monica Mountains from time to time. Though it is rare to spot one, if you do, make yourself appear as large as possible. Do not crouch down, run, or make any sudden movements.

- Rattlesnakes are the only kind of snake you might come across that is likely to pose any danger. They are most commonly seen in the warmest months when they may be sunning themselves on warm rocks. If you see a rattlesnake, pass it at a distance if it is sitting still or patiently allow it to pass if you see it on the move.

- Ticks are the last bit of "wildlife" of any concern. Tick bites put you at risk of contracting Lyme disease. After hiking in vegetative areas, be sure to check yourself and especially your dog for ticks. If you do find any, pull them out completely using tweezers.

Plants

Though most of the plants you will spot in this area will be chaparral and wildflowers, poison oak is not uncommon. Poison oak can be found along many of the trails in this book, as well as along the rivers and creeks running through the area and at parks and campgrounds. Poison oak can be especially daunting in the winter because the stems are bare, making the plant much harder to identify. Familiarize yourself with what poison oak looks like (remember the rule: leaves of three, let it be) before you go and avoid it as best as you can.

Zero Impact

Trails in West LA are heavily used year-round. We, as trail users and advocates, must be especially vigilant to make sure our passage leaves no lasting mark. Here are some basic guidelines for preserving trails in the region:

- Pack out all your own trash, including biodegradable items like orange peels. You might also pack out garbage left by less considerate hikers.

- Don't approach or feed any wild creatures—the ground squirrel eyeing your snack food is best able to survive if it remains self-reliant.

- Don't pick wildflowers or gather rocks, antlers, feathers, and other treasures along the trail. Removing these items will only take away from the next hiker's experience.

- Avoid damaging trailside soils and plants by remaining on the established route. This is also a good rule of thumb for avoiding poison oak and other common regional trailside irritants.

- Don't cut switchbacks, which can promote erosion.

- Be courteous by not making loud noises while hiking.

- Many of these trails are multiuse, which means you'll share them with other hikers, trail runners, mountain bikers, and equestrians. Familiarize yourself with the proper trail etiquette, yielding the trail when appropriate.

- Use outhouses at trailheads or along the trail.

How to Use This Guide

This guide is designed to be simple and easy to use. Each hike is described with a map and summary information that delivers the trail's vital statistics including length, difficulty, fees and permits, park hours, canine compatibility, and trail contacts. Directions to the trailhead are also provided, along with a general description of what you'll see along the way. A detailed route finder (Miles and Directions) sets forth mileages between significant landmarks along the trail.

Hike Selection

The hikes listed in this book range from leisurely strolls to more challenging hikes. You will find hikes that range in distance from 1 mile to 6 miles, across varying terrain. Whether you are visiting for a weekend, or a local of many years, you should find a hike in this book to serve your interests. There are excellent options for getting a good workout, as well as options that are best for days when you just want to get outside without too much effort. It is important to remember that while we believe these are the best easy day hikes in the area, not every hike is right for every person. Be sure to check out the trail finder to help you choose the right hike for you and your hiking partners.

Difficulty Ratings

These are all easy hikes, but easy is a relative term. A fit runner may find a 3-mile, hilly hike easy, while some may expect easy to be short and flat. First-time hikers and sea-soned veterans likely also have different expectations. So to aid in the selection of a hike that suits your particular needs and abilities, each hike is rated easy, moderate, or more challenging. Bear in mind that even the most challenging routes can be made easy by hiking within your limits and taking rests when you need them.

- **Easy** hikes are generally short and/or have little elevation gain, usually taking no more than an hour to complete.

- **Moderate** hikes involve more elevation gain, and may require slightly more coordination than the easy hikes, often crossing streams or scrambling over rocks.

- **More challenging** hikes feature some steep stretches and greater distances, and generally require more fitness and technical skills.

These are completely subjective ratings—consider that what you think is easy is entirely dependent on your level of fitness and coordination, and the adequacy of your gear. If you are hiking with a group, you should select a hike with a rating that's appropriate for the least fit and prepared in your party.

Approximate hiking times are based on the assumption that on flat ground, most walkers average 2 to 3 miles per hour. Adjust that rate by the steepness of the terrain and your level of fitness (subtract time if you're an aerobic animal and add time if you're hiking with kids), and you have a ballpark hiking duration. Be sure to add more time if you plan to picnic or take part in other activities like bird watching or photography.

Trail Finder

Map Legend

═══⟨10⟩═══	Interstate Highway
═══⟨101⟩═══	U.S. Highway
═══⟨1⟩═══	State Highway
───────	Local Road
= = = = = =	Unpaved Road
▬▬▬▬▬▬	Featured Trail
- - - - - - -	Trail
⁓⁓⁓	River/Creek
⬭	Body of Water
⛌	Bridge
∧	Cave
🅿	Parking
🛆	Picnic Area
■	Point of Interest/Structure
👥	Ranger Station
🚻	Restroom
▒▒▒▒▒	Steps
○	Town
❶	Trailhead
⬟	Viewpoint/Overlook
❓	Visitor Center
≋	Waterfall

1 Escondido Falls

This trail winds its way past towering Malibu mansions and through Escondido Canyon, roughly following the creek. After 2 delightfully flat miles, the trail ends at a tranquil travertine rock pool at the base of a 50-foot waterfall.

Distance: 4 miles out and back
Approximate hiking time: 1.5 hours
Difficulty: Easy
Trail surface: Road, dirt trail
Best season: Year-round, though the waterfall is best in the rainy season
Other trail users: Mountain bikers

Canine compatibility: Leashed dogs permitted
Fees and permits: No fees or permits required
Schedule: Any time
Maps: USGS Point Dume
Trail contacts: Santa Monica Mountains Conservancy; (310) 589-3200; www.smmc.ca.gov

Finding the trailhead: From Highway 1, also known as the Pacific Coast Highway, drive north to Winding Way. Winding Way is approximately 15 miles from Santa Monica. There is no traffic light here so look for the street sign on your right. Turn right on Winding Way and park in the parking lot on the left side of the road. GPS: N 34' 01.564 / W 118' 46.808

The Hike

This creekside hike hidden in the base of the canyon begins by leaving the parking area and walking up the road past multimillion-dollar mansions. There is a dirt trail that follows alongside the road as you begin the only climb of the hike. After a short climb the road heads back downhill and winds its way into the canyon.

After 0.8 mile you'll pass a bulldozed trail on your left. Continue down the road another 200 yards to where the road ends behind a chained gate with a sign indicating the Edward Albert Escondido Canyon Trail. Continue a short ways past the gate and at the 1-mile mark, the gravel road ends and becomes a wide dirt trail. Just past the dirt turnoff, the trail forks. Take the left fork into Escondido Canyon. The right fork leads toward the neighboring Latigo Canyon. Shortly after the fork you will cross the creek for the first time. At 1.1 mile cross the creek again and take the left fork on the opposite side of the creek. At 1.2 miles continue straight at the fork and follow the trail as it winds back and forth, crossing the creek a number of times.

At 1.5 miles you will reach another fork. The left fork crosses over the creek. Stay straight to stay on the right side of the creek. Continue to follow the creek until you reach a final fork at 1.6 miles. Take the left fork to head toward the waterfall. From here you will catch a glimpse of the falls up ahead, and this is actually the only spot along the trail where you will see two waterfalls—the one you are about to reach and another larger falls above it. The upper falls are about 150 feet tall. Continue on another 0.4 mile and the trail will emerge at the falls. This lower falls is about 50 feet tall and most impressive during the rainy months. In summertime it is possible to find the falls nothing more than a dry rock face, though the creek will be running year-round. The upper and lower falls combined make the tallest waterfall in the Santa Monica Mountains. Take a dip in the pool at the base of the falls before turning around and heading back out the way you came.

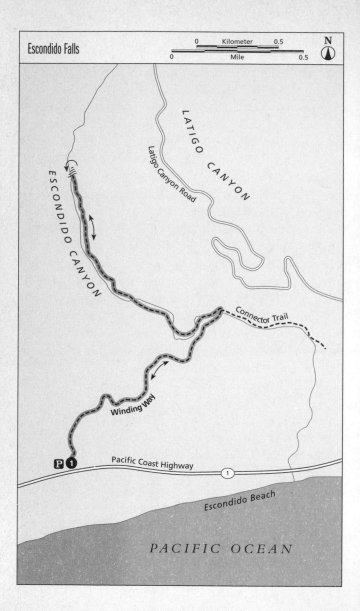

Escondido Falls

Kilometer
0   0.5
Mile
0   0.5

N

LATIGO CANYON

Latigo Canyon Road

ESCONDIDO CANYON

Connector Trail

Winding Way

Pacific Coast Highway

1

P 1

Escondido Beach

PACIFIC OCEAN

Miles and Directions

0.0 Begin at the parking area at Winding Way. Follow the road up away from Pacific Coast Highway.

0.8 Pass a bulldozed trail on your left and continue down the road. Then pass a chained fence marking the end of the road and see the sign on your left indicating the Edward Albert Escondido Canyon Trail.

1.0 The road becomes a dirt trail. Reach the fork and take the left fork.

1.1 Cross the creek. Then cross the creek again. Once across, take the left fork.

1.2 Reach another fork and stay straight.

1.4 Arrive at a fork and take the right fork.

1.5 Cross the creek again and then stay straight at the fork shortly after the creek.

1.6 Arrive at another fork and take the left fork.

2.0 Arrive at the waterfall. Turn around and retrace your steps back.

4.0 Arrive back at the parking area.

2 Point Dume

As iconic Southern California as it gets, the Point Dume hike begins at a popular beach and traverses up a cliff overlooking the Malibu coastline. Simply take in the view while watching the surfers and rock climbers below, or make your way down to the beach to explore the tidepools.

Distance: 1.3 miles out and back

Approximate hiking time: 1 hour

Difficulty: Easy

Trail surface: Dirt trail, sandy path

Best season: Year-round

Other trail users: Surfers, rock climbers, tidepoolers

Canine compatibility: Dogs not permitted

Fees and permits: No fees or permits required; however, a parking fee is required for state beach parking lot.

Schedule: Sunrise to sunset

Maps: USGS Point Dume

Trail contacts: Point Dume State Beach; (310) 457-8144; www .parks.ca.gov

Finding the trailhead: From Santa Monica, take Pacific Coast Highway west to Westward Beach Road. Turn left on Westward Beach Road to enter Point Dume State Park. Drive all the way through the park and past the fee collection kiosk. Park at the end of the parking lot and you will find the trailhead directly south of the cul-de-sac. GPS: N 34' 00.183 / W 118' 48.560

The Hike

At the end of Westward Beach Road lies the Point Dume State Beach, a popular place for filming movies (scenes from *D-Day the Sixth of June, Planet of the Apes,* and *Iron Man* were all filmed here). This hike begins by crossing a spectacular section of Malibu beach. Begin the hike by finding the trail at the end of the cul-de-sac and follow it across the sand toward the bluff. At the base of the bluff you will likely see rock climbers. A number of excellent single-pitch climbs can be done here with spectacular views from the face of the bluff.

Follow the trail up the side of the bluff. These bluffs initially were bare, covered only sparsely by chaparral. But after World War II, locals planted trees and non-native plants that now cover the hillside. In the springtime, the bluffs are littered with wildflowers. Follow the trail and go right at the fork at 0.1 mile. Take another right at 0.2 mile to continue toward a viewing platform. Here you could also take a left if you wanted to hike to the summit of the bluff. Continue straight and at 0.4 mile you will reach a viewing platform directly below the summit. To the right you can see Point Dume Beach and to the left is Pirates Cove. From December through March, you may also catch a view of the grey whales migrating for the winter.

Continue on past the viewing platform and the trail will become a boardwalk. At 0.5 mile take a right to continue on the trail. From here you could also turn left to head up the backside to the summit. From atop the summit you'll notice the rocky triangle that the point creates. What you are standing on is made of black volcanic rock whereas the rock on either side of the point is white sedimentary rock. The volcanic rock is heartier and withstands the beating of the sea better than the softer white rock, and therefore has held its ground while the white rock has receded around it creating a point.

Skip the summit for now, and at 0.6 mile there is a staircase on your right-hand side leading down to the beach.

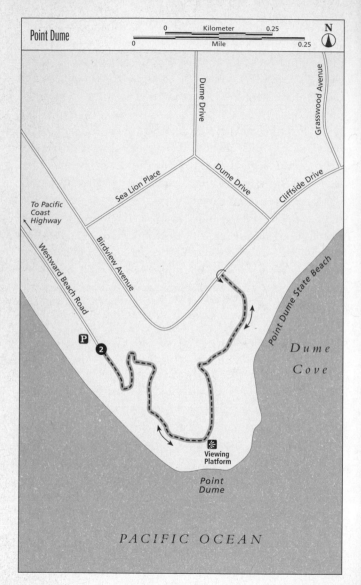

Point Dume

0 Kilometer 0.25
0 Mile 0.25

N

Grasswood Avenue

Dume Drive

Sea Lion Place

Dume Drive

Cliffside Drive

To Pacific
Coast
Highway

Westward Beach Road

Birdview Avenue

Point Dume State Beach

P
2

Dume
Cove

Viewing
Platform

Point
Dume

PACIFIC OCEAN

Head down to the beach to explore the tidepools or at low tide, walk along the beach for a mile to Paradise Beach. Paradise Beach can be a great place to get some privacy—something hard to come by on a California beach. There is also a popular restaurant at Paradise Beach where you can grab a meal or a cocktail before heading back. If you choose not to head down to the tidepools or Paradise Beach, you can continue straight on the trail or turn left and the trail will end at the street. Turn around here and head back the way you came or wind along any of the alternate routes heading back over the bluffs.

Miles and Directions

0.0 Walk to the end of the parking lot and continue across the sand toward the bluffs. Find the trail on your left.

0.1 Arrive at a fork and stay to the right.

0.2 Arrive at another fork and stay to the right.

0.4 Arrive at a viewing platform. Continue on the trail on the boardwalk.

0.5 Turn right at the fork to head toward the beach. (The left trail here will lead you to the peak of the dunes.)

0.6 Arrive at a fork. Turn left to stay on the trail, or you can turn right and head down the staircase to the beach and tide-pools below.

0.65 The trail ends at the street. Turn around here and retrace your steps or wander on one of the many additional forks, all giving you different views of the coastline.

1.3 Arrive back at the trailhead.

3 Temescal Canyon

Beginning at Temescal Gateway Park, this hike gently rises up alongside Temescal Creek before entering Topanga State Park. The trail passes a small waterfall before heading up the hillside. Atop the crest of this hike are sweeping views of Malibu and the skyscrapers of downtown Los Angeles.

Distance: 3.1-mile loop
Approximate hiking time: 1.5 hours
Difficulty: Moderate due to elevation gain
Trail surface: Dirt trail
Best season: Year-round, though the waterfall may be best after a rain and the trail can get hot in the heat of summer
Other trail users: Joggers

Canine compatibility: Dogs not permitted
Fees and permits: Parking fee required
Schedule: Dawn to dusk
Maps: USGS Topanga
Trail contacts: Temescal Canyon Park, 15601 Sunset Blvd., Pacific Palisades, 90272; (310) 840-2187 or (310) 454-1395; www.lamountains.com

Finding the trailhead: From Santa Monica, take Pacific Coast Highway north to Temescal Canyon Road. Turn right on Temescal Canyon Road and continue 1 mile toward Sunset Boulevard. Enter the park just after passing Sunset Boulevard and park in the lot. GPS: N34' 03.222 / W118' 31.725

The Hike

One of the more popular hiking destinations of West LA, the hike through Temescal Canyon can get crowded, but if you time it right, you can get an excellent workout and spectacular views for a rare peaceful moment amid the buzz of Los Angeles. Begin by walking through the parking area and then on through the Temescal Canyon Conference and Retreat Center. After a short ways on a gravel road you will pass a metal chain across a path. Continue on, onto the dirt road. Here there are a few short trails that traverse the conference center grounds and then enter Temescal Gateway Park. Temescal Gateway Park is a 141-acre park filled with oaks, sycamores, and scenic vistas, owned and operated by the Santa Monica Mountains Conservancy since 1994. From this park, you can follow trails to access both Topanga State Park directly to the west as well as Will Rogers State Park to the east.

Continue straight ahead on the main trail through the middle of the retreat and after half a mile the trail emerges from a shady meadow and begins the climb toward a waterfall. At 0.8 mile you will see a sign indicating you are entering Topanga State Park. The trail does not change dramatically when crossing the line that divides the parks, but bear in mind that leashed dogs *are* allowed in the Temescal Gateway Park, while dogs are *not* allowed in Topanga State Park. So if you plan to hike past the first 0.8 mile, be sure to leave your four-legged pal at home.

After the sign the trail narrows and climbs up a shady hillside following Temescal Creek. Surrounded by oak and maple trees, continue the gentle climb until at 1.2 miles you reach a wooden bridge crossing the creek. There is a small waterfall here that is not particularly impressive, but it is a nice spot to take a break or a photo nonetheless. Across the bridge to continue the climb up toward Temescal Ridge. At 1.6 miles the trail forks and you can continue straight to hike on Trailer Canyon Trail to Skull Rock—a large windswept sandstone boulder that you can sit atop and take in the views, or take a left to head up Temescal Ridge to a lookout point and then loop back down to the trailhead.

Continuing up the Temescal Ridge Trail, at 1.6 miles you catch first sight of a view. Malibu will be off to your right along with a fork for the Bienvenda Trail. Continue straight toward the crest of the ridge. At the crest at 1.8 miles you'll have amazing views of Los Angeles. In one 360-degree turn, you can see all that is LA: the high rises of downtown, the sweeping coastline, and the palm trees and mansions of Malibu. Continue on to the clearing at 1.9 miles and turn left to begin your descent.

Continue taking left forks as you follow the switchbacks descending the ridge with intermittent views of beaches and mansions. At 3 miles the trail intersects with the ascending trail along with a number of others. Here you will turn right to head back toward the conference center and on to the parking area.

Miles and Directions

0.0 Begin at the parking area at Temescal Gateway Park and walk through the grounds of the Temescal Canyon Conference and Retreat Center.

0.3 Follow the gravel then dirt road past the chained path.

0.5 Emerge from a shady meadow and begin a gradual ascent.

0.8 Pass the sign noting your entrance into Topanga State Park. This sign will tell you the waterfall is 0.4 mile ahead.

1.2 Reach the seasonal waterfall and cross the wooden bridge.

1.3 Reach a fork and turn right.

1.5 Turn right, following a steep rock face on your left.

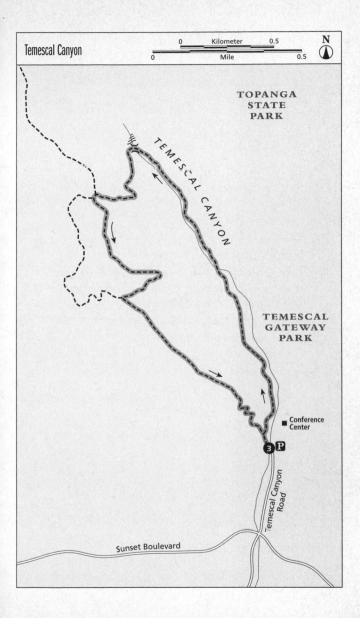

Temescal Canyon

0   Kilometer   0.5
0   Mile   0.5

N

TOPANGA
STATE
PARK

TEMESCAL CANYON

TEMESCAL
GATEWAY
PARK

Conference
Center

3 P

Temescal Canyon Road

Sunset Boulevard

1.6 Reach the junction with the Trailer Canyon Trail. Continue straight to head to Skull Rock, or turn left following the sign to Sunset Boulevard, to continue on the Temescal Ridge Trail on the loop back to the parking area.

1.7 Reach a junction with the Bienvenda Trail to your right. Continue straight.

1.8 Reach the crest of the ridge and take in the spectacular 360-degree view.

1.9 Reach a clearing. Take the trail on your left.

2.2 Reach another junction with the Bienvenda Trail. Take the left fork.

2.4 Reach a fork. Take the left fork.

2.6 Reach another small clearing. Take the trail on your left and begin switchbacks down the ridge.

3.0 Reach a fork where the trail meets up with a number of other trailheads beginning at the conference center. Turn right to head back toward the conference center. Take the staircase on your left leading back down to the road.

3.1 Arrive back at the parking area.

4 Santa Ynez Canyon

This flat hike begins on an easy trail through a lush canyon, before branching off the main trail and following the creek. After a short ways following the creek, you can boulder hop the last few hundred feet upstream as the canyon walls narrow before finally reaching a small 18-foot waterfall sitting in a peaceful sandstone alcove.

Distance: 2.2 miles out and back
Approximate hiking time: 1.5 hours
Difficulty: Easy followed by moderate boulder hopping at the end
Trail surface: Dirt trail, rocky riverbed
Best season: Year-round, but the waterfall is at its best in the winter

Other trail users: None
Canine compatibility: Dogs not permitted
Fees and permits: No fees or permits required
Schedule: Sunrise to sunset
Maps: USGS Topanga
Trail contacts: Topanga State Park; (310) 455-2465

Finding the trailhead: From Santa Monica, drive north on Pacific Coast Highway to Sunset Boulevard. Turn right and drive 0.4 mile to Palisades Drive. Turn left on Palisades Drive and continue approximately 2.5 miles to a residential street called Vereda de la Montura. Turn left and follow the road to where it dead-ends. Park on the street just before the gated community. GPS: N34' 04.688 / W118' 34.042

The Hike

You might be surprised to find such a lovely little slice of wilderness beginning amid a giant housing development in the middle of Pacific Palisades. You may be even more surprised that this hike is in this book, when you spot the graffitied concrete channel at the start of the hike. Rest assured, suburbia and graffiti both fall away quickly, leaving you with an easy and charming trail.

Begin this hike by walking through the iron gate and down the stairs. The trail passes over a paved waterway and then continues to snake its way across the creek two more times. At 0.25 mile there is a neat small cave on your right. Continue on the trail following on the east side of the creek. Shortly after the cave you will cross the creek three more times—the last time picking up the trail slightly up ahead and on your right. At 0.5 mile you will reach a fork. Stay to the right and continue on to the signed junction with the Trippet Ranch Trail. To hike to Trippet Ranch you would take the left fork. You can also begin this hike at Trippet Ranch for a longer 6-mile trek to the waterfall. For the sake of an easy day hike, take the right fork leading to a very narrow, almost hidden, trail toward the falls.

Cross the creek at 0.6 mile and pick the trail up on your left. From here you are simply going to follow the creek upstream. There are a number of smaller trails here that follow along the creek as well as some that lead away from it. Take any path you choose as long as you continue to follow the creek. At some points it may be easier to walk directly in the creek, while in other places, the trail will be very obvious and well maintained. You will essentially need to cross the creek four times before you begin the final 150-foot approach to the waterfall.

At 1 mile the canyon walls narrow and the trail is lost in the creek. From here you can boulder hop your way up toward the falls. Just before the falls there is a steep rock about 8 feet high. Scale it on your own or use the knotted rope affixed to the side to pull yourself up. Shortly beyond this

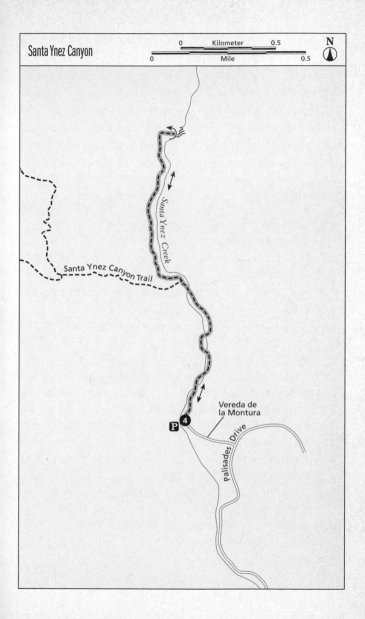

Kilometer

0   0.5

Mile

0   0.5

N

Santa Ynez Creek

Santa Ynez Canyon Trail

P 4

Vereda de
la Montura

Palisades Drive

climb is the 18-foot-high Santa Ynez Falls. Though I hear it can be quite impressive during the rainy months, its power is reduced to a trickle in the warmer months. However, despite the lack of water, this small rock grotto has a surprising amount of charm. You can turn around here or you can actually continue up over the falls via another fixed rope on the left-hand side of the falls. Three more rope climbs will take you into the canyon to where the trail disappears.

Miles and Directions

0.0 Begin at the trailhead on Vereda de la Montura, walking through the metal gate and down the stairs.

0.1 Cross the paved waterway. Quickly cross the creek two more times.

0.2 See the small cave on your right. Continue down the trail.

0.3 Cross the creek. Then cross the creek again.

0.5 Cross the creek again. Find the trail up ahead on the right. Stay to the right at the fork.

0.6 Arrive at a post indicating the trail to Trippet Ranch to the left and the waterfall to the right. Head to the right on the narrow trail toward the creek and cross the creek. Take the trail on your left heading upstream.

0.8 Cross into the creek, follow in the creek bed, and pick the trail back up on the right side.

0.9 Cross the creek to the left, continue shortly ahead, then cross the creek back to the right.

1.0 Boulder hop the last 150 feet toward the falls. Just before the falls climb up the fixed rope on the left side of the canyon.

1.1 Arrive at the base of the falls.

2.2 Arrive back at the trailhead.

5 **Solstice Canyon**

Take a walk through wilderness and history on an easy walk up to ruins. Have a picnic by the serene waterfall before beginning an excellent workout up the ridge and finishing your hike with a nice long downhill with sweeping ocean views.

Distance: 2.9-mile loop
Approximate hiking time: 1.5 hours
Difficulty: Moderate
Trail surface: Paved road, dirt road, trail
Best season: Year-round
Other trail users: Joggers
Canine compatibility: Leashed dogs permitted

Fees and permits: No fees or permits required
Schedule: Any time
Maps: USGS Point Dume, USGS Malibu Beach
Trail contacts: Santa Monica Mountains National Recreation Area Visitor Center, 401 W. Hillcrest Dr., Thousand Oaks, 91360; (805) 370-2301; www .nps.gov/samo

Finding the trailhead: From Santa Monica, take Highway 1 west to Corral Canyon Road. Turn right and drive 0.2 mile to the entrance to Solstice Canyon. Turn left and drive 0.3 mile to the parking area. You will first pass the overflow parking area. Continue past this to the main parking area at the trailhead. GPS: N34' 02.275 / W118' 44.851

The Hike

Solstice Canyon is filled with a variety of different options for hikes of varying length and difficulty. One of the best ways to experience the canyon is to hike the Solstice

Canyon Trail to the Rising Sun Trail. Begin by hiking straight on the road from the parking area. You will pass a staircase on your right that will be your return trail. Continue straight up the paved road following the creek. After a short ways, you will pass an intersection with a road on your right and a trail branching off to your left. Continue straight on the Solstice Canyon Trail. After passing another trail branching off to your right, you will come to an intersection with a dirt road. Turn right to continue up toward the Tropical Terrace.

At 0.6 mile you will pass the ruins of an old stone house on your right. This is the ruin of the Keller House. Rancher Henry Keller built this house in 1903 as a hunting cabin. After the original cabin built on this site was burned in a wildfire, Keller built this home out of stone in order to withstand the wildfires that frequently ravaged this area. The construction did survive many years, but ultimately perished in the Corral Fire of 2007. The remnants can be seen just across the creek.

Continue on this trail and you will pass a bridge on your right. Stay straight as the dirt road becomes single-track. From here the trail forks, and either fork takes you up the trail a short ways before meeting back up. Continue straight ahead on the trail and at 1.1 miles the Sostomo Trail branches off on your left. You can take this trail to explore the upper reaches of the canyon, but for the sake of this book, we are going to continue straight ahead. At 1.2 miles you will reach what is known as the Tropical Terrace. In 1952 this home was designed by architect Paul Williams for Fred and Florence Roberts. The home was designed to incorporate all of the natural features surrounding it, like the creek that runs through it and the waterfall cascading just feet away. This home was burned in a fire in 1982 but the foundation remains for your exploration.

Just past the Tropical Terrace, pass a refreshing waterfall on your left and continue across the creek up to the Rising Sun Trail. Here the workout really begins as you climb up the ridge on switchbacks. At 1.7 miles you will catch your first glimpse of the Pacific Ocean views that will lure you back to the trailhead. Continue along the ridge as it climbs and then eventually descends onto a paved parking area. This is actually the former site of a TRW research facility that tested groundbreaking space technology until the facility eventually closed in 1973. Much of the remains of this operation were burned in the 2007 wildfire.

Turn left through this paved lot and find the trail on your right. At 2.7 miles turn left at the fork to continue back to the trailhead. Cross the road and arrive at the trailhead at just under 3 miles.

Miles and Directions

0.0 Begin by hiking past the parking area up the paved road.

0.2 Pass a road on your right that leads to the Rising Sun Trail, a trail on your left that leads to the TRW loop, and a picnic area on your left. Continue straight.

0.3 Pass another intersection on your right. Continue straight until you reach the fork in the road. Turn right and continue ahead on the dirt road.

0.6 Across the creek on your right side, see the ruins of the Keller House.

0.7 Come to a bridge on the right side of the trail. Continue straight until you come to a fork where the dirt road becomes singletrack. Take either fork.

0.8 Cross the creek.

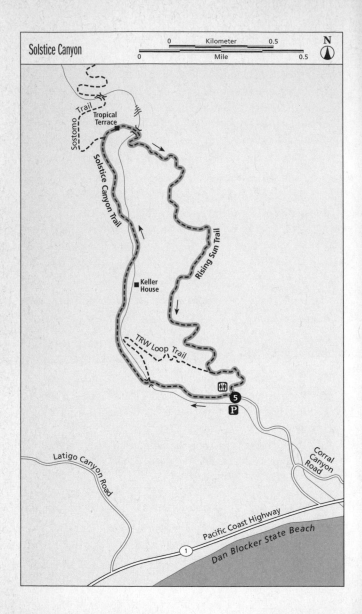

Solstice Canyon

Sostomo Trail

Tropical Terrace

Solstice Canyon Trail

Keller House

Rising Sun Trail

TRW Loop Trail

5
P

Latigo Canyon Road

Corral Canyon Road

Pacific Coast Highway

1

Dan Blocker State Beach

Kilometer
0   0.5

Mile
0   0.5

N

0.9 Cross the creek again.

1.1 Arrive at a fork with the Sostomo Trail on your left. Continue straight.

1.2 Arrive at the Tropical Terrace. Explore the ruins before continuing back on the trail and passing the creek with a waterfall on your left. Continue straight ahead on the Rising Sun Trail.

1.7 After climbing up switchbacks, arrive at a peak with nice ocean views.

2.6 The trail descends onto the site of the former TRW research facility. Turn left through the paved area and find the trail on your right-hand side.

2.7 Arrive at an intersection. Turn left.

2.9 Arrive back at the trailhead.

6 Malibu Creek State Park

A popular day trip from Los Angeles or the San Fernando Valley, this hike takes you on an easy walk to a picturesque swimming hole and then past the crowds to the lesser visited but equally stunning Century Lake. You will pass through a number of locations used in filming TV shows and movies including *Planet of the Apes* and the *Swiss Family Robinson*.

Distance: 3.6 miles out and back

Approximate hiking time: 1.5 hours

Difficulty: Easy to the rock pool, moderate from the pool to the lake

Trail surface: Fire road

Best season: Year-round, but it can get very hot and crowded in the peak of summer

Other trail users: Joggers

Canine compatibility: Dogs not permitted

Fees and permits: Parking fee required

Schedule: Dawn to dusk

Maps: USGS Malibu Beach

Trail contacts: Malibu Creek State Park; (818) 880-0367; www.parks.ca.gov

Finding the trailhead: From Santa Monica, drive west on Highway 1 until you reach Malibu Canyon Road. Drive 6.5 miles and you will see the entrance to Malibu Creek State Park on your left. Pay the fee at the kiosk and drive to the last day use parking area. GPS: N34' 05.802 / W118' 42.995

The Hike

This spectacular hike provides perhaps some of the best scenery with some of the least effort of all of the hikes in this area. For this reason, Malibu Creek State Park can get awfully crowded on warm, sunny weekends, which can, of course, lessen the beauty. But if you can hit it on a weekday or on an uncharacteristically empty day, this may very well become your favorite refuge from the city. The flat dirt road makes this hike great for families with kids, and you could even take a jogging stroller on this path if you wanted to—although if you do take a stroller, you may want to skip the last quarter mile to the swimming hole as it is on more uneven, singletrack terrain. Formerly owned by Bob Hope, Ronald Reagan, and 20th Century Fox, this land was predominantly used for filming (the site of the TV show *M*A*S*H* is just a short ways past the end of this hike) until it was acquired by Malibu Creek State Park in 1974. Now camera crews still occasionally join the hordes of nature seekers here.

Begin this hike by crossing the lower parking lot and walking down the stairs leading to the creek. Cross the creek and continue straight on the dirt road. After a short ways, you will pass the Grassland Trail on your right. Continue straight on the dirt road. At 0.3 mile there will be a fork on your left. Stay straight on Crags Road, also known as High Road. Continue winding your way through the canyon and at 0.8 mile you will see a small trail leading off to your left. Continue straight another 0.1 mile to a three-way intersection. At the intersection you will see a bridge to your left leading to the visitor center. The visitor center is open from noon to 4:00 p.m. on weekends. Turn left toward the bridge but just before crossing the bridge, take the trail on your right to follow the creek.

At 1 mile you will find yourself at another three-way intersection. Take the fork on the far left and begin walking

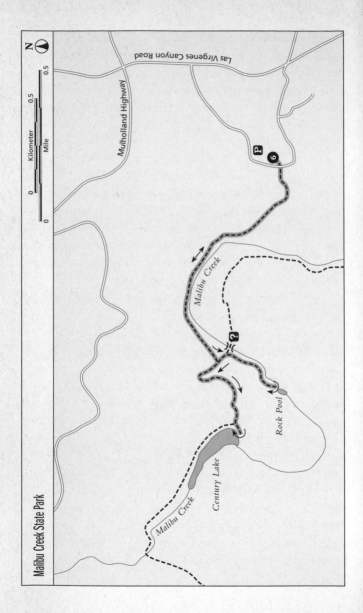

Malibu Creek State Park

Las Virgenes Canyon Road

Mulholland Highway

Malibu Creek

Century Lake

Malibu Creek

Rock Pool

Kilometer

0   0.5

Mile

0   0.5

N

down the singletrack trail along the creek. You will pass by a rock wall on your right where you can often see climbers scaling the wall where scenes from *Planet of the Apes* were filmed. Just past the wall the trail will wind around and dead-end at a large pool surrounded by high rock walls—former home to many scenes from the *Swiss Family Robinson*.

After you have had your share of swimming, head back out toward the main dirt road. When you reach the bridge, make a left and another left to continue uphill on Crags Road. Climb your way up for half a mile before reaching Century Lake on your left. This can be a nice shady refuge from a hot day in the sun. From here, turn around and hike back out the way you came.

Miles and Directions

0.0 Begin by hiking through the parking lot down the stairs toward the creek.

0.2 See the Grassland Trail on the right. Continue straight.

0.3 See a trail forking off to the left. Continue straight on Crags Road.

0.8 A trail branches off to your left. Continue straight.

0.9 Arrive at a three-way intersection. Turn left to walk toward the bridge. Just before the bridge turn right and hike along the trail following the creek. If you would like to stop at the visitor center, you can go straight across the bridge to get there.

1.0 At a three-way intersection, take the fork on the far left that descends farther toward the creek.

1.2 Arrive at the rock pool. Turn around here and head back out to the bridge.

1.4 Back at the intersection by the bridge, turn left and then left again back onto Crags Road. Follow the road uphill.

1.9 Just beyond the crest of the hill, see a small trail heading off the main road on your left. Follow this trail down toward the lake.

2.0 Arrive at the lake. Turn around here, hike back up to Crags Road, and follow the road all the way back down to the trailhead.

3.6 Arrive back at the trailhead.

7 Canyon View Trail/Ocean View Trail Loop

An uphill trek through the chaparral–ridden lower Zuma Canyon leads you to an excellent lookout point where you can see all the way from Point Dume to Palos Verdes on a clear day. After a tough workout you start your leisurely descent back into the canyon while looking for wildlife and enjoying the cool ocean breezes.

Distance: 3.2-mile lollipop
Approximate hiking time: 1.5 hours
Difficulty: Moderate due to short but steep uphill climb
Trail surface: Singletrack path
Best season: Year-round, although it can get quite hot in the peak of summer
Other trail users: Equestrians

Canine compatibility: Leashed dogs permitted
Fees and permits: No fees or permits required
Schedule: Any time
Maps: USGS Point Dume
Trail contacts: Santa Monica Mountains Visitor Center, 401 W. Hillcrest Dr., Thousand Oaks, 91360; (805) 370-2301; www .nps.gov/samo

Finding the trailhead: From Santa Monica, drive west on Highway 1 to Bonsall Drive. Turn right on Bonsall Drive and go 1 mile to where the road turns into a narrow dirt road. Continue on the dirt road until it dead-ends in a large dirt parking area. Find the trailhead on the northeast end of the parking lot. GPS: N34' 01.903 / W118' 48.723

The Hike

Stretching from the ocean up to Mulholland Drive, Zuma and Truncas Canyons together make up over 13,000 acres and are home to a great deal of wildlife, with private property speckled throughout. May Rindge and her husband, Frederick, bought the property back in 1892 and are greatly responsible for its current undeveloped state. While they adamantly declared that no roads be built throughout, after twenty years of fighting, the Supreme Court demanded that they allow a road to pass through, thus creating what is now known as Highway 1, or Pacific Coast Highway. Though May might be horrified to know the traffic that now traipses through her once quiet land, the rest of us are happy to have access to all of the excellent land up and down the Malibu coast.

There are some very long and arduous hikes traversing this area, though you can get much of the beauty with a lot less perspiration by hiking the Canyon View and Ocean View Trails. Head out from the dirt parking lot up the trail and you will pass the Zuma Loop Trail on your left followed by the Ocean View Trail on your right at 0.2 mile. The Ocean View Trail will be your return route, but for now, continue up the Zuma Canyon Trail a bit farther, crossing a creek and arriving at a fork with the Canyon View Trail at 0.5 mile. Turn right here to leave the wide trail and begin your uphill climb on the singletrack. The trail will arc around the ridge before peaking at a viewpoint at 1.6 miles. At 1.8 miles you will meet up with Kanan-Edison Road, which is actually nothing more than a dirt trail, and there is a sign here indicating the Zuma Canyon connector. Continue straight a short ways farther and at 1.9 miles turn right at the sign for the Ocean View Trail. Wind your way downhill until the trail meets back up with the Zuma Canyon Trail. Turn left and walk back to the trailhead.

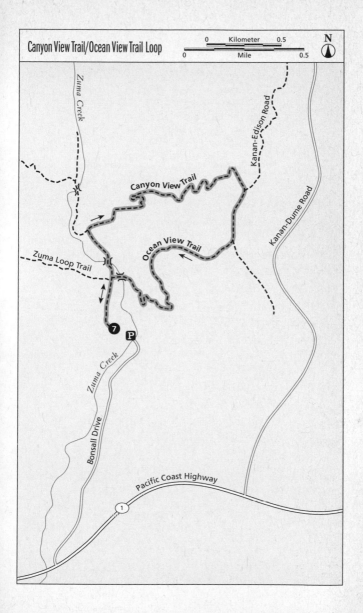

Canyon View Trail/Ocean View Trail Loop

0   Kilometer   0.5

0   Mile   0.5

N

Zuma Creek

Kanan-Edison Road

Canyon View Trail

Ocean View Trail

Kanan-Dume Road

Zuma Loop Trail

7   P

Zuma Creek

Bonsall Drive

Pacific Coast Highway

1

Miles and Directions

0.0 Begin at the trailhead at the northeast end of the parking lot.

0.2 Pass the intersection with the Zuma Loop Trail on the left. Continue straight. Pass the intersection with the Ocean View Trail on your right. Continue straight.

0.3 Cross the creek.

0.5 Come to an intersection with the Canyon View Trail. Turn right off the main trail to head up the Canyon View Trail.

1.6 Arrive at a peak with views of the Pacific.

1.8 See a fork on your left with a sign saying ZUMA CANYON CONNECTOR. Continue straight.

1.9 Arrive at a fork with the Ocean View Trail. Take the right fork to head down the Ocean View Trail.

2.9 Cross the creek.

3.0 Arrive back at the Zuma Canyon Trail and turn left to head back toward the trailhead.

3.2 Arrive back at the parking area.

8 Inspiration Point Loop

Take a stroll through the property of former Hollywood star Will Rogers while taking in the views, exploring his old homestead, and maybe even taking in a polo match. Hike on the miles of trail that loop through the property or hike up and connect to the famous Backbone Trail—a 64-mile trail traversing the Santa Monica Mountains.

Distance: 2.1-mile loop
Approximate hiking time: 1 hour
Difficulty: Easy
Trail surface: Dirt road, forested trail
Best season: Year-round
Other trail users: Joggers, cyclists
Canine compatibility: Leashed dogs permitted
Fees and permits: Parking fee required

Schedule: Trails are open any time, though ranch house tours are Mon-Fri 11:00 a.m., 1:00 p.m., and 2:00 p.m., and Sat-Sun 10:00 a.m.–4:00 p.m. every hour.
Maps: USGS Topanga
Trail contacts: Will Rogers State Historic Park, 1501 Will Rogers Park Rd., Pacific Palisades, 90272; (310) 454-8212; California State Parks; (800) 777-0369; www.parks.ca.gov

Finding the trailhead: From Westwood, take the 405 freeway north and exit at Sunset Boulevard. Drive 7 miles west to Will Rogers State Park Road. Turn right and follow the road to the park entrance. Stop at the parking kiosk to purchase your parking pass and park in the lot just behind the kiosk, or continue straight ahead and park in front of the polo field. GPS: N34' 03.265 / W118' 30.703

The Hike

Will Rogers was a man of many talents. After great success as a performer on Broadway, Rogers moved to Hollywood to pursue his career in acting. A successful and wealthy man, he bought a 186-acre ranch where he and his family could relax on weekends. Shortly thereafter, they moved to the ranch to live full-time. In 1944, nine years after Rogers's untimely death in a plane crash, his wife left the land and the home to the State of California, ensuring it would be protected and enjoyed for years to come. The thirty-one-room ranch house still stands and is kept in its original condition for visitors to tour. The polo field was built to indulge his love of horses, and matches are still played here on weekends.

Once you have toured the home, caught a polo match, or picnicked on the extensive lawns outside the house, begin your hike by walking through the parking lot back toward the entrance. Just past the tennis courts on your right, turn right and follow the trail up the switchbacks made of stairs. At 0.2 mile the trail intersects a fire road. Turn left onto the fire road and begin the Inspiration Loop Trail.

Continue straight as you pass a trail on your left at 0.4 mile. At 0.7 mile a small singletrack trail branches off the fire road on your right. Turn right to head toward the trail's namesake, Inspiration Point. The trail gets significantly prettier here as the crowds of the main trail dissipate and the views open up to the canyon. At 0.9 mile you will come to a small fork. Turn left to head up some wooden steps before arriving at the lookout. Here you will find a large plateau with a few benches where you can stop for a picnic. To continue on the loop, walk straight across the viewing area

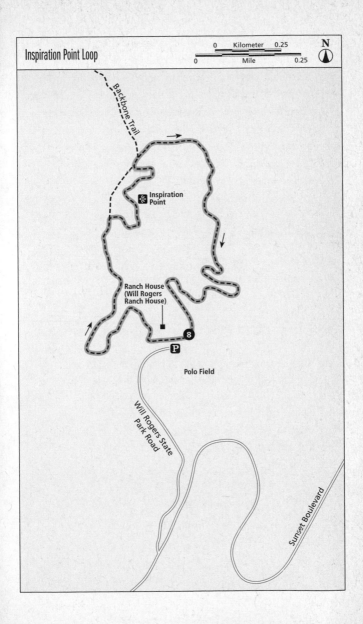

Inspiration Point Loop

0   Kilometer   0.25
0   Mile   0.25

N

Backbone Trail

Inspiration Point

Ranch House
(Will Rogers
Ranch House)

8

P

Polo Field

Will Rogers State
Park Road

Sunset Boulevard

and pick up the trail on the other side. After a short down-hill on the trail you will meet back up with the fire road. Turn right to continue the loop back toward the trailhead. At 1.1 miles you will see a small turnoff on your left leading to the Backbone Trail, a 64-mile-long trail from east to west through the Santa Monica Mountains.

Continue on the main fire road as it curves its way around the hillside. Stay straight at the signed junction at 1.5 miles. At 2 miles, turn left onto the road and continue back to the parking area.

Miles and Directions

0.0   Begin at the parking lot heading west past the ranch house.

0.1   Turn right just past the tennis courts and hike up the switch-backs to the fire road. Turn left on the main fire road.

0.4   Stay straight as you pass a small trail on your left.

0.7   Turn right, leaving the main trail and heading toward Inspira-tion Point.

0.9   Arrive at a fork and turn left to hike up the stairs and arrive at Inspiration Point. Continue through the plateau and find the trail on the other side. Begin a short descent.

1.0   Arrive back at the main trail and turn right.

1.1   See the Backbone Trail branching off on your left, climbing up a steep incline. Stay straight on the main trail.

1.2   Pass a trail on your right. Continue straight.

1.5   Continue straight at the signed junction.

2.0   Arrive at a road and turn left to walk back toward the park-ing area and the polo field.

2.1   Arrive back at the parking area.

9 Getty View Trail

This conveniently located trail climbs a steep slope up to a ridge overlooking the lush Hoag Canyon. From the top of the ridge you can turn left or right for views of the famous Getty Museum, the Pacific Ocean, and the canyon.

Distance: 2.2 miles out and back

Approximate hiking time: 1 hour

Difficulty: Moderate due to steep uphill climb

Trail surface: Dirt trail, dirt road

Best season: Year-round

Other trail users: None

Canine compatibility: Leashed dogs permitted

Fees and permits: Parking fee required

Schedule: Sunrise to sunset

Maps: USGS Beverly Hills

Trail contacts: Santa Monica Mountains Conservancy; (310) 589-3200; www.smmc.ca.gov

Finding the trailhead: From West LA, drive north on the 405 freeway and exit at Getty Center Drive. Turn left onto Sepulveda Boulevard. The parking area to the trailhead is just ahead on the right side. GPS: N34' 05.800 / W118' 28.575

The Hike

The trailhead's great accessibility creates a trade-off; its proximity to I-405 means you get views of the freeway for much of the first half of the hike. But if you can tune out the traffic and look just beyond the lanes, you can get stunning views along with a great workout, all easily accessible without any windy driving. Begin by finding the trail on the north side of the parking lot and begin your hike uphill.

Follow the narrow trail up the switchbacks on the west side of the canyon. At 0.3 mile there is a small fork. Turn

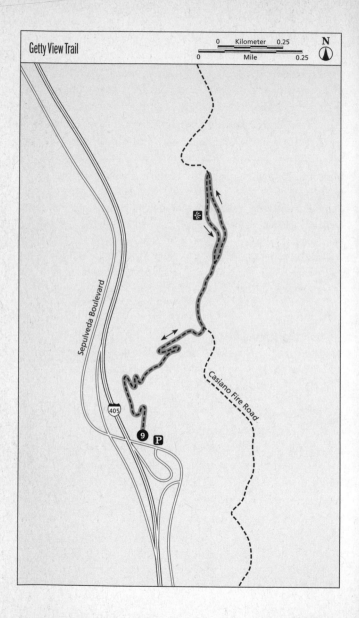

Getty View Trail

Sepulveda Boulevard

405

9 P

Casiano Fire Road

0 Kilometer 0.25

0 Mile 0.25

N

right and continue up the trail. At 0.7 mile the trail crests the ridge at a fire road. From here you can turn right and continue along the ridge for half a mile to the south. For the sake of this hike, we will instead turn left and follow the ridge to the north. Walk along the fire road here above Hoag Canyon. At 0.9 mile there is a small trail branching off to the left leading up to a viewpoint. Continue on the main road and you can visit this spot from the opposite side on the return hike. Continue on and at 1.1 miles the trail will disappear into a residential neighborhood. Turn around just before the trail curves west and you will see a small trail leading up a small ridge on your right. Take this trail up toward a lookout point; just be prepared to scratch your legs or your dog's nose just a bit as this trail is narrow and riddled with spiky brush.

At 1.2 miles you will reach the crest of the overlook and continue on down the other side. Meet back up with the road and retrace your steps back down the hillside.

Miles and Directions

0.0 Find the trailhead on the north end of the parking lot.

0.3 Arrive at a small fork. Turn right.

0.7 Arrive at a junction with a dirt road. Turn left and head north.

0.9 Pass a small trail on your left.

1.1 Just before the trail curves west and enters the residential neighborhood, turn around and start heading back. Find a small offshoot trail on your right and head up the incline.

1.2 Arrive at the overlook. See the Getty Museum up ahead across the freeway. Continue down the other side of the trail.

1.3 Meet back up with the road and turn right. Continue back down the way you came.

2.2 Arrive back at the trailhead.

10 Cold Creek Canyon Preserve

This hike travels down into the Cold Creek Canyon amid a unique array of plants and wildlife. From this shady trail you can see wildflowers like stream orchids and scarlet monkey flowers and pass by the ruins of an old house carved from sandstone.

Distance: 3.1 miles out and back
Approximate hiking time: 1.5 hours
Difficulty: Moderate
Trail surface: Dirt trail
Best season: Year-round
Other trail users: none
Canine compatibility: Dogs not permitted
Fees and permits: A free visitor's

permit is required and can be obtained by calling the Mountains Restoration Trust at (818) 591-1701.
Schedule: Dawn to dusk
Maps: USGS Malibu Beach
Trail contacts: Mountains Restoration Trust, 3815 Old Topanga Canyon Road, Calabasas, 91302; (818) 591-1701; www .mountainstrust.org

Finding the trailhead: From Santa Monica, drive west on Pacific Coast Highway to Malibu Canyon Road. Turn right on Malibu Canyon Road. Drive 6.5 miles and turn right on Mulholland Highway. Continue 4 miles to Stunt Road and turn right. Drive along Stunt Road and at 3.3 miles you will see the gated entrance to the preserve on your left. You will need to drive up a short ways to make a U-turn and park along the shoulder of the road. GPS: N34' 05.059 / W118' 39.131

The Hike

Owned by the Mountains Restoration Trust, this 1000–acre preserve is predominantly maintained by volunteers. Floods, fires, and earthquakes are constantly wreaking havoc on the area, changing the configuration of the trails, destroying and re-growing wildlife, and even changing the route of the creek running through it. The preserve endured flooding most recently in 1994 and previously in 1970 and 1943. Since 1994 the trails have been restored so they can be enjoyed. The hike begins atop a ridge and steadily descends into the bowl of the canyon. Remember that what goes down, must come up, so be prepared for a workout on your way back out of the canyon.

This hike begins by passing through the metal gate on Stunt Road. There is only one main trail that passes through the preserve, and they ask that you do not attempt to bush-whack your way along any of the obviously unkempt trails for fear of upsetting the harmony of the existing landscape. Make your way on the narrow trail through the low-hanging canopy of trees and brush. At 0.5 mile the trail passes by an old rusty truck. During one of the many fires that endangered this area, someone was driving the truck down to a stone house farther down the trail to evacuate more items, when the fire overtook the truck and the driver leapt from the car and ran for safety. The driver's life was spared but the truck did not fare as well and its remnants are still on the trail.

At just under 1 mile, you will pass the ruins of an old stone house on the left. This house was initially inhabited by Herman Henthke between 1910 and 1920. After Hen-thke left, presumably to marry his next wife, the Murphy family moved into the house. After surviving several fires and rebuilding the house numerous times, the fire of 1970 finally caused Mrs. Murphy to say "enough," and she trans-ferred the property to The Nature Conservancy, who later transferred it to the Mountains Restoration Trust.

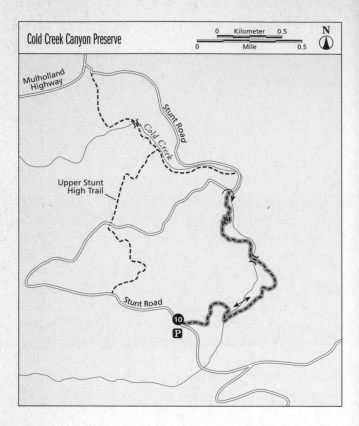

Continuing a short ways past the house you will cross over a small bridge with a lovely cascade flowing. Continue descending farther down into the canyon and eventually, at 1.5 miles, you will reach the locked gate at the opposite end of the preserve. This is your turnaround point.

Miles and Directions

0.0 Begin by walking through the gate on the northeast side of the road.

0.4 Cross a small wooden bridge over a seasonal creek.

0.5 Pass the rusty remains of a truck alongside the trail.

0.8 Cross another small wooden bridge over the creek.

1.0 Cross over another small bridge with water cascading down the rocks on your right.

1.1 Begin switchbacks heading up the hillside. While the majority of the hike in is descending, this small portion is ascending.

1.5 See a signpost on your left. Turn left and continue on until you reach the locked gate at the opposite end of the preserve. Turn around here and head back the way you came.

3.1 Arrive back at the trailhead.

11 Red Rock Canyon Park

Reminiscent of the Southwest, this hike takes you past numerous sandstone rock formations as you make your way through this unique park. After passing a series of caves that you can walk through, sit in, or climb over, the hike ends at a stunning overlook among heaps of sandstone boulders.

Distance: 2.4 miles out and back

Approximate hiking time: 1 hour

Difficulty: Moderate due to some elevation gain

Trail surface: Dirt road and dirt trail

Best season: Year-round, though it can get quite hot in the summer months with little shade on the trail

Other trail users: Equestrians

Canine compatibility: Leashed dogs permitted

Fees and permits: Parking fee required

Schedule: Sunrise to sunset

Maps: USGS Malibu Beach

Trail contacts: Santa Monica Mountains Conservancy; (310) 589-3200; www.smmc.ca.gov.

Finding the trailhead: From Santa Monica, head west on Pacific Coast Highway to Topanga Canyon Boulevard. Turn right on Topanga Canyon Boulevard and drive 5 miles to Old Topanga Canyon Road. Turn left on Old Topanga Canyon Road and drive 1.9 miles to Red Rock Road. Turn left and follow the road until it dead-ends at a dirt parking lot at the trailhead. GPS: N34' 06.372 / W118' 38.228

The Hike

The Red Rock Trail can be accessed from a few different trailheads. You can hike this trail beginning on Stunt Road at the trailhead for the Calabasas Peak Trail if you want a longer, more challenging hike. For the sake of this book and for the sake of an easy day hike, we start this hike from Red Rock Canyon Park. You will drive through a quaint residential neighborhood on a narrow dirt road to find the park hidden in the canyon. After parking in the dirt parking lot, continue up the road on foot. At 0.2 mile you will pass some great caves on your left. Explore these before continuing a short ways farther up the road. At 0.4 mile take the small footpath off to your right. If you were to continue on this dirt road, it would go on for another 0.8 mile before meeting up with the Calabasas Peak Trail. Turn right off the main road and begin your ascent by climbing up the wooden steps. At 0.6 mile there is the first of many overlooks on your right. A bit farther at 0.8 mile, there is another series of interesting caves on your right. Climb around them, take a break from the sun in their shade, or continue on straight ahead.

At 1 mile there is a small overlook on your right. Continue straight on the trail as it continues to climb up the ridge before ending in a giant cluster of rich red sandstone boulders. Turn around here and hike back the way you came.

Miles and Directions

0.0 Begin by walking through the parking area and continuing up the dirt road.

0.2 Pass by a cluster of intricate cave systems on your left.

0.4 Find the Red Rock Trail, a small offshoot trail on your right. Turn right and walk up the wooden steps.

0.6 Check out the overlook point on your right.

0.8 Pass by another cluster of interesting rock formations, just slightly off the trail on your right. Continue straight on the trail.

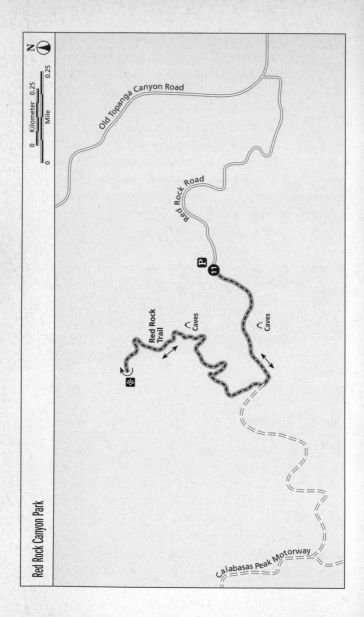

Red Rock Canyon Park

Old Topanga Canyon Road

Red Rock Road

P
11

Red Rock Trail

Caves

Caves

Calabasas Peak Motorway

N

0   Kilometer   0.25
0   Mile   0.25

1.0 Pass by a small offshoot trail on your right that leads to an overlook point.

1.2 Arrive at a large cluster of massive sandstone boulders that sit atop a peak. Admire the view, explore the caves, and then turn around here and retrace your steps back to the trailhead.

2.4 Arrive back at the trailhead.

12 Baldwin Hills Scenic Overlook

See Los Angeles in a new light from atop the 500-foot peak at the new Baldwin Hills Overlook. After stopping at the state-of-the-art visitor center, wander through the fifty acres of restored natural habitats and enjoy the views, the picnic tables, and the workout.

Distance: Hiker's choice of a variety of trails, up to 2 miles total

Approximate hiking time: 30 minutes to 1 hour

Difficulty: Easy

Trail surface: Dirt path

Best season: Year-round

Other trail users: None

Canine compatibility: Dogs not permitted

Fees and permits: No fees or permits required

Schedule: 8:00 a.m. to sunset. Visitor center open select weekend hours.

Maps: USGS Hollywood

Trail contacts: Baldwin Hills Conservancy, 5120 Goldleaf Circle, Suite 290, Los Angeles, 90056; (323) 290-5270; www .parks.ca.gov/bhso

Finding the trailhead: From the 10 freeway, take the Robertson exit in Culver City. Continue straight as it becomes Exposition Boulevard. Go 0.4 mile and take the slight left onto Venice Boulevard. Drive 0.2 mile to National Boulevard. Turn right on National Boulevard and drive 0.7 mile to West Jefferson Boulevard. Turn right and drive 0.7 mile to Hetzler Road. Turn left on Hetzler Road and follow the road up the hillside until it dead-ends at the Baldwin Hills Overlook parking area. GPS: N34' 00.958 / W118' 22.934

The Hike

The new Baldwin Hills Scenic Overlook was opened in April of 2009 by the Baldwin Hills Conservancy and the

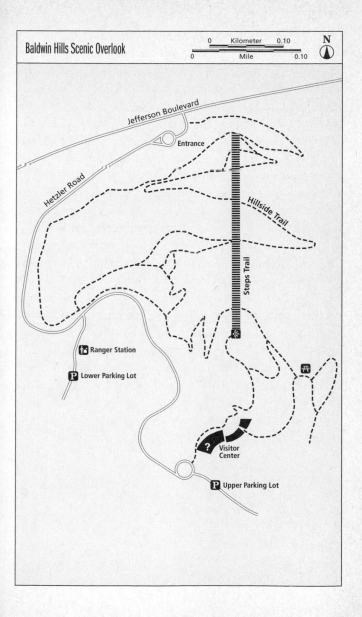

Baldwin Hills Scenic Overlook

0   Kilometer   0.10
0   Mile   0.10

N

Jefferson Boulevard

Entrance

Hetzler Road

Hillside Trail

Steps Trail

Ranger Station

P Lower Parking Lot

? Visitor Center

P Upper Parking Lot

LA County Parks and Recreation Department, adding fifty more acres of land to explore in Culver City. After driving up a winding road, you emerge up top at the visitor center. Park your car here and first spend some time at the visitor center. This modern building is filled with displays exhibiting the local ecology and native plant species, as well as the history of the area including fires and construction. After you have had your fill of education, begin the hike on the trail just outside of the visitor center.

Hike past the visitor center and the additional conference room buildings and continue straight ahead to a viewpoint at 0.1 mile. From here you can turn back around and at 0.2 mile, make a left turn. Throughout the preserve you can take any number of trails to explore views from different angles, and you can even choose to hike down a very long and steep staircase to the base of the hill, or take a long winding trail that follows the road, to hike down via a slightly more sane trip. You could also simply wander the endless loops and enjoy some time at the picnic tables.

At 0.25 mile you can make a right turn to head to some picnic tables, or turn left to walk toward the top of the staircase. At 0.3 mile you will see the very long and steep staircase leading down to your right, or you can continue straight ahead to take the trail that follows the road.

13 Parker Mesa Overlook

This uphill climb follows an easy to follow fire road up into the hills of Topanga State Park. The wide trail winds through chaparral with views of the ocean and the park. After a great 2-mile workout, turn off the main trail for the final ascent onto Parker Mesa Overlook. A bench with a view marks the turnaround of this scenic yet challenging hike.

Distance: 5.2 miles out and back

Approximate hiking time: 2 to 2.5 hours

Difficulty: Moderate due to hefty uphill climb, exposed on sunny days

Trail surface: Fire road, dirt trail

Best season: Year-round, though it can get hot in the peak of summer

Other trail users: Joggers

Canine compatibility: Dogs not permitted

Fees and permits: No fees or permits required

Schedule: Any time

Maps: USGS Topanga

Trail contacts: Topanga State Park, (310) 455-2465, www .parks.ca.gov

Finding the trailhead: From Santa Monica, take Pacific Coast Highway west to Sunset Boulevard. Turn right on Sunset Boulevard and drive 0.3 mile to Paseo Miramar. Turn left on Paseo Miramar and wind your way up this steep road through a residential neighborhood. Follow the road to where it dead-ends at the trailhead and park anywhere you can find a spot along the road. Don't forget the emergency brake! GPS: N34' 03.050 / W118' 33.421

The Hike

Within the Los Angeles city limits lies Topanga State Park, a parkland covering over 36 miles of trail. Considered to be the largest wildland in the world that lies completely within the boundaries of a major city, Topanga Park stretches from east to west from Rustic Canyon to Topanga Canyon and consists of fire roads and singletrack trails, many with spectacular ocean and city center views. The Parker Mesa Overlook Trail is no exception.

Beginning in an upscale Pacific Palisades neighborhood, the hike begins off Paseo Miramar at the end of the road where the fire road begins at a metal gate. You could also begin this hike off Los Liones for a slightly longer hike, beginning with an extra mile of singletrack. For the sake of an easy day hike, we start at the fire road off Paseo Miramar and immediately begin the uphill climb. This wide trail will wind its way up the hillside, and at 0.25 mile you will reach a junction with a narrow trail on your left. This is the Los Liones Trail that you could have begun your hike on if you wanted a more rigorous, 7-mile adventure. Continue past this junction, staying on the fire road, and follow the trail as it winds farther up the mountain. At 0.4 mile and again at 0.5 mile there will be nice viewpoints on your right.

Continue on and the trail will continue to climb before leveling out briefly and then climbing again. At 2.1 miles you will reach an intersection. The right fork would lead another 2.5 miles along the East Topanga Fire Road to Trippet Ranch and the main visitor center and trailhead of Topanga State Park. Instead, take the left fork and continue on 0.5 mile to where the trail ends at an open landing with a bench, marking the Parker Mesa Overlook. Take in the 360-degree views before heading back for a downhill hike back to the trailhead.

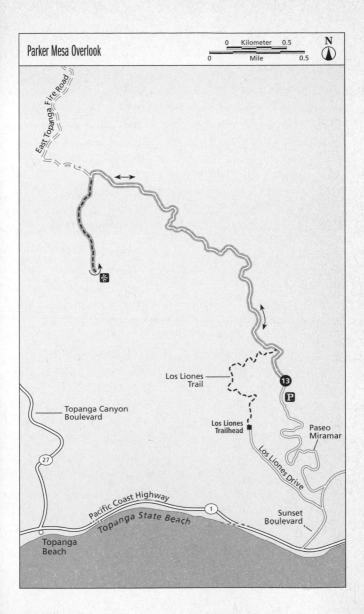

Parker Mesa Overlook

0   Kilometer   0.5
0   Mile   0.5

N

East Topanga Fire Road

Los Liones Trail

Topanga Canyon Boulevard

27

Los Liones Trailhead

13

P

Paseo Miramar

Los Liones Drive

Sunset Boulevard

Pacific Coast Highway

1

Topanga State Beach

Topanga Beach

Miles and Directions

0.0 Begin at the end of Paseo Miramar on the dirt road.

0.2 Arrive at a fork with the Los Liones Trail on the left. Continue straight ahead on the Topanga Fire Road.

0.4 Arrive at a fork with an overlook on your right. Continue straight ahead on the fire road.

0.5 Arrive at a fork with an overlook on your right. Continue straight ahead on the fire road.

2.1 Arrive at a fork. Take the left fork onto a narrower trail and head south.

2.6 Arrive at a wide, open clearing marking the Parker Mesa Overlook. Turn around here.

5.2 Arrive back at the trailhead.

14 Dead Horse Trail

This short but interesting hike begins at Trippet Ranch and meanders through chaparral, sandstone, and multiple species of ferns. On this relatively flat trip you will cross over a creek on a rustic bridge before reaching your turnaround at the Dead Horse parking area.

Distance: 2.5 miles out and back

Approximate hiking time: 1 hour

Difficulty: Easy due to relatively flat terrain and easy to follow trail

Trail surface: Dirt trail

Best season: Year-round

Other trail users: Joggers

Canine compatibility: Dogs not permitted

Fees and permits: Parking fee required.

Schedule: 8:00 a.m. until dusk

Maps: USGS Topanga

Trail contacts: Topanga State Park; (310) 455-2465; www .parks.ca.gov

Finding the trailhead: From Santa Monica, head west on Pacific Coast Highway and turn right on Topanga Canyon Boulevard Drive 4.6 miles to just past the funky yet charming town of Topanga and turn right on Entrada Road. Follow Entrada Road as it climbs uphill and twists and turns through a neighborhood. At 0.7 mile turn left staying on Entrada Road, following the signs toward Trippet Ranch. Drive 0.3 mile and turn left again heading into the Trippet Ranch parking area. Drive into the parking area and turn right. Park anywhere. GPS: N34' 05.619 / W118' 35.282

The Hike

The Dead Horse Trail is a quiet trail that meanders through the outskirts of Topanga State Park. Though the official

Dead Horse trailhead begins just off Topanga Canyon Boulevard, this entrance and parking area was indefinitely closed at the time of this writing and thus the Topanga Canyon Boulevard trailhead actually becomes the destination. The trailhead for this hike is at Trippet Ranch. Trippet Ranch was formerly a gentlemen's club, used as a refuge from the city. Now the ranch boasts a large parking area, restrooms, and picnic tables. A number of different trails begin or end here. From Trippet Ranch you can access the Santa Ynez Trail, the Topanga Fire Road, the Eagle Springs Fire Road, the Musch Trail, or of course, the Dead Horse Trail.

Find the trailhead leading toward the Musch Trail on the northeast end of the parking lot. Take the fire road about 50 feet before a narrow trail intersects on the left-hand side. Turn left off of the main trail and onto the Dead Horse Trail. As you hike along a field on your right and a forest on your left, you will come to a junction at 0.3 mile. Continue straight ahead and at 0.4 mile you will reach another fork. This time take a right to continue toward the Dead Horse parking area. After a gradual descent into the valley, you will come to a bridge at 0.9 mile. This bridge was built across the creek in 1986 and has a rustic charm unique to this area.

After crossing the bridge you will reach a three-way fork at 1 mile. Take the middle fork to continue toward the Dead Horse trailhead. Continue to follow the signs that say TRAIL until you reach a final fork at 1.25 miles. The right fork leads you down to the Dead Horse parking area where you can utilize the picnic tables before heading back up and out the way you came.

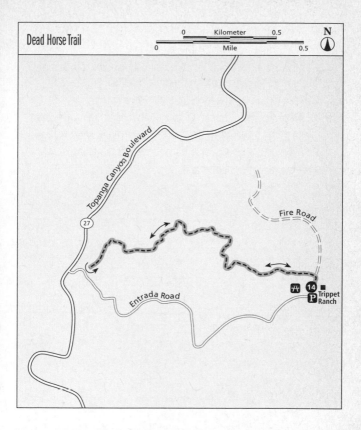

Miles and Directions

0.0 Begin at the Trippet Ranch parking area and head north on the Musch Trail. Turn left off of the main road and onto the Dead Horse Trail.

0.3 Arrive at a fork. Continue straight ahead.

0.4 Arrive at a fork. Turn right.

0.9 Cross the creek on the bridge.

1.0 Arrive at a three-way junction. Take the middle fork and then shortly thereafter arrive at another fork. This time take the right fork, following the sign that says TRAIL.

1.2 Arrive at a fork. Continue straight ahead. At the next fork, go right and descend to the Dead Horse parking area.

1.3 Arrive at the Dead Horse parking area. Turn around here.

2.5 Arrive back at Trippet Ranch.

15 Newton Canyon Falls

This short canyon trail follows a portion of the Backbone Trail past the seasonal Newton Creek, ending at the 30-foot-tall Newton Canyon Falls. Though the falls will be dry in the summer months, the hike still makes for a very peaceful trip, culminating at a rocky grotto, perfect for picnicking.

Distance: 1 mile out and back
Approximate hiking time: 45 minutes
Difficulty: Easy
Trail surface: Dirt trail
Best season: Year-round, though the falls are only flowing during the winter months
Other trail users: Joggers
Canine compatibility: Leashed dogs permitted

Fees and permits: No fees or permits required
Schedule: Any time
Maps: USGS Point Dume
Trail contacts: Santa Monica Mountains National Recreation Area Visitor Center, 401 W. Hillcrest Dr., Thousand Oaks, 91360; (805) 370-2301; www .nps.gov/samo

Finding the trailhead: From Santa Monica, drive west on Highway 1 to Kanan-Dume Road. Turn right on Kanan-Dume Road and drive 4.4 miles. The trailhead will be on your left just after the first tunnel. Park in the dirt parking lot by the sign that says BACKBONE TRAIL. GPS: N34' 04.563 / W118' 48.940

The Hike

Stretching over 64 miles through the Santa Monica Mountains, perhaps the most notable monument throughout the region, is the Backbone Trail. The Backbone Trail runs

Newton Canyon Falls

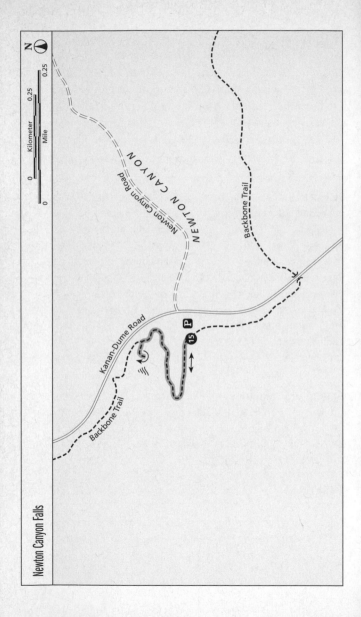

N

Kanan-Dume Road

Newton Canyon Road

NEWTON CANYON

Backbone Trail

Backbone Trail

P **15**

Kilometer
0   0.25

Mile
0   0.25

east-west traversing from Will Rogers Park to the east, to Point Mugu to the west. With campgrounds scattered every few miles, the entire length of the Backbone Trail can make for an excellent weeklong backpacking trip. But if you don't have the time or inclination to rough it to quite this extent, segments of the famous trail can still be enjoyed easily in a day, or even in as short a time as an hour. It is not uncommon for hikers to shuttle cars and hike 4- to 7-mile segments as a point-to-point, though there are ways to enjoy it with even less distance or logistical support. Newton Canyon Falls is one such place.

Beginning at the well-marked trailhead, follow the shaded path as it descends into Newton Canyon, roughly following the direction of Kanan Road above. At 0.4 mile take the left-hand fork off of the main trail. Go approximately 50 yards and you will reach a three-way fork. Take the small fork on your left and follow it a few yards until it dead-ends at the top of the falls. If the falls are running and you want to see them in their entirety, head back to the three-way fork and turn left. Follow this trail 0.1 mile and you will be able to work your way down into the grotto at the base of the falls on your left.

There are a number of small trails here you can choose to take if you are looking for a longer hike or a better workout. Continuing on the trail following downriver, the trail will climb back up away from the riverbank where it will eventually reconnect with the Backbone Trail. From here you can hike on as long as you wish.

Miles and Directions

0.0   Begin at the trailhead off Kanan Road with a sign indicating the Backbone Trail.

0.4   Arrive at a small fork. Turn left to hike toward the river. Continue on and arrive at a three-way fork. Turn left to continue to the top of the falls. Turn around here or continue on to the base of the falls.

1.0   Arrive back at the trailhead.

16 Venice Canals

Initially built by Abbot Kinney to be the Venice, Italy, of the United States, little is left of the 16 miles of canals that once ran through the heart of Venice Beach, but what is left is more than a mile of beautiful waterway, lined by some of the most exclusive homes in the area. A stroll alongside the canals and over the wooden bridges makes for a nice walk only a few short blocks from the famous Venice Beach boardwalk.

Distance: 1.3 miles or more, depending on how you choose to walk it

Approximate hiking time: 45 minutes

Difficulty: Easy

Trail surface: Paved path

Best season: Year-round, though the beauty of the area is enhanced in the sunshine

Other trail users: None

Canine compatibility: Leashed dogs permitted

Fees and permits: No fees or permits required, though you will likely have to pay for parking

Schedule: Any time

Maps: USGS Venice

Trail contacts: City of Los Angeles Department of Recreation and Parks; Park Ranger Hotline (323) 644-6661; www.laparks.org/Venice

Finding the trailhead: From Santa Monica, head south on Pacific Avenue. Turn left on Venice Boulevard. There is a large parking lot on Venice Boulevard where you can park for $12. You could also look for street or metered parking on any of the streets bordering the canals on Washington Boulevard, Pacific Avenue, or Dell Avenue. From Dell Avenue at Venice Boulevard, walk south to enter the canals. GPS: N33' 59.231 / W118' 27.944

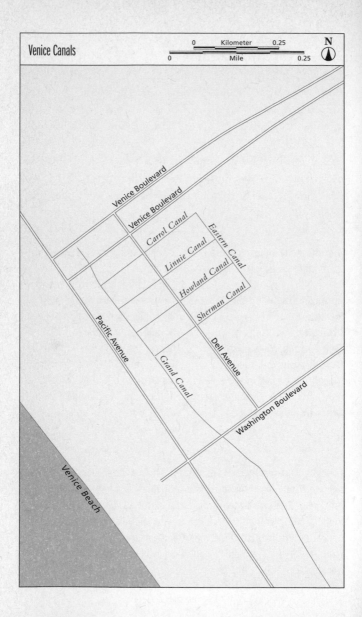

Venice Canals

0   Kilometer   0.25

0   Mile   0.25

N

Venice Boulevard

Venice Boulevard

Carrol Canal

Eastern Canal

Linnie Canal

Howland Canal

Sherman Canal

Pacific Avenue

Dell Avenue

Grand Canal

Washington Boulevard

Venice Beach

The Hike

In 1904, millionaire Abbot Kinney directed the digging of 16 miles of canals through the Venice Beach area, intending to mimic the canals of Venice, Italy, and to drain the wet, marshy area that he was building a new town on. However, the canals were built during the horse and buggy era, and once cars were commonplace, the canals were no longer practical as the cars could not navigate the narrow paths and bridges traversing the area. In 1929, in order to accommodate the onslaught of automobiles, the majority of the canals were filled in to become roads. After falling into disrepair in the 1950s, the canals have since been restored to their original beauty. The most recent facelift was in 1993, when the canals got new sidewalks and refurbished canal banks. Today there are six canals remaining; visitors can wander along the banks and over the bridges. Approximately 370 single-family homes call the canals home and make for some excellent real estate ogling.

You can begin your walk from any border of the canals. If you begin your walk from Dell Avenue and Venice Boulevard, head south to the first canal, Carrol Canal. Turn left to walk down Carrol Canal to where it ends at Eastern Canal. Follow Eastern Canal south as it passes three additional canals. You can traverse back down any of these canals. If you continue down Eastern Canal, it will make a right turn at Sherman Canal. Follow Sherman Canal or any other to where they end at Grand Canal. Cross over Grand Canal on one of its three bridges and walk the entire length of Grand Canal to where it ends at Washington Boulevard. Follow your steps back to the car or take any alternate route of canals and bridges to make your way back.

17 Franklin Canyon Lake

This short but tranquil hike passes by Heavenly Pond before skirting the perimeter of the nineacre Franklin Canyon Lake, and then crossing back to finish the hike along the shores of the lake under shady tree canopies.

Distance: 0.6-mile loop
Approximate hiking time: 45 minutes
Difficulty: Easy
Trail surface: Paved road, dirt path
Best season: Year-round
Other trail users: None
Canine compatibility: Leashed dogs permitted

Fees and permits: No fees or permits required
Schedule: Dawn to dusk
Maps: USGS Beverly Hills
Trail contacts: Franklin Canyon Park Visitor Center, 2600 Franklin Canyon Dr., Beverly Hills; (310) 858-7272; www.la mountains.com

Finding the trailhead: From Beverly Hills, take Sunset Boulevard to Beverly Drive. Head north on Beverly Drive and drive 0.6 mile to a fork. Turn left at the fork to continue on Beverly Drive. Continue 0.8 mile on Beverly Drive before the road curves to the right onto Franklin Canyon Drive. Drive 1.8 miles through Franklin Canyon Park before arriving at the Sooky Goldman Nature Center parking lot. Continue past the parking lot. Follow the one-way road 0.2 mile and park in any of the dirt parking areas along the road or in the lot at the start of the Wodoc Nature Trail. GPS: N34' 07.288 / W118' 24.678

The Hike

Franklin Canyon Park is a 600–acre park in the heart of Los Angeles broken up into two sections: Upper Franklin

Canyon and Lower Franklin Canyon. Easily accessible from Beverly Hills, you can head here for a day excursion to hike the various trails or simply enjoy the picnic areas. Franklin Canyon Lake and Heavenly Pond, both located in the Upper section of the park, are on the Pacific flyway—the route of migrating birds—so the bird watching here can be impressive.

The lake is manmade and was originally built in 1914 as a collaborative effort between William Mulholland and the City of Los Angeles Department of Water and Power as a reservoir to distribute the water that was brought into LA from the north. But in 1971 after the Sylmar earthquake, its structural soundness was questioned and it was taken out of use as a reservoir. Surrounded by much undeveloped land in the midst of sprawling Los Angeles, this area was quickly slated for development, but thanks to the persuasive arguments of conservationist Sooky Goldman and Congressman Howard Berman, the land instead became a park. The National Park Service purchased the area in 1981 as part of the forming Santa Monica Mountains National Recreation Area.

This hike begins at the Wodoc Nature Trail, a paved walkway taking you a short ways around Heavenly Pond. In only 0.1 mile, you will see dozens of turtles. Once around the pond you will meet back up with the main road. Continue across the dam and down the stairs to a dirt path. Follow the dirt path as it winds its way around Franklin Canyon Lake. Once around the lake, you can take any of the wooden staircases leading back up to the road. From here it will be just a short walk back to your car.

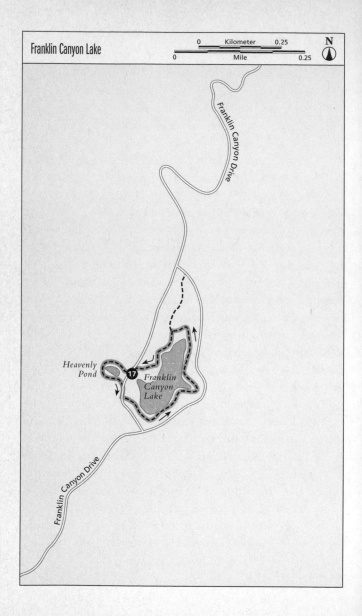

Franklin Canyon Lake

N

0   Kilometer   0.25
0   Mile   0.25

Franklin Canyon Drive

Heavenly
Pond

17

Franklin
Canyon
Lake

Franklin Canyon Drive

Miles and Directions

0.0 Begin at the signed trailhead of the Wodoc Nature Trail on the right side of the road. Follow the trail counterclockwise around the pond. Look out for turtles!

0.1 Arrive back at Franklin Canyon Drive. Turn right and continue on the road across the dam.

0.2 Once across the dam, turn left off the road and head down the wooden staircase. Continue straight on the dirt path as it winds around the reservoir.

0.4 Arrive at a concrete spillway. Cross the spillway. Once across, turn left to continue along the opposite side of the lake.

0.5 Take any of the wooden staircases back up to Franklin Canyon Drive. Turn left and continue back to the Wodoc trailhead.

0.6 Arrive back at the trailhead.

18 Franklin Canyon Park: Hastain Trail/Discovery Trail Loop

In the lower portion of Franklin Canyon Park, combine these two diverse trails for a perfect mix of challenging uphills, sweeping views, and leisurely flats. Hike the loop in just under 2 miles or extend your hike by adding a side trip to a viewpoint for a 2.6-mile round trip.

Distance: 1.8-mile loop
Approximate hiking time: 1 hour
Difficulty: Moderate due to some uphill climbing
Trail surface: Fire road, dirt trail
Best season: Year-round
Other trail users: None
Canine compatibility: Leashed dogs permitted

Fees and permits: No fees or permits required
Schedule: Dawn to dusk
Map: USGS Beverly Hills
Trail contact: Franklin Canyon Park Visitor Center, 2600 Franklin Canyon Dr., Beverly Hills, 90210; (310) 858-7272; www .lamountains.com

Finding the trailhead: From Beverly Hills, take Sunset Boulevard to Beverly Drive. Head north on Beverly Drive and drive 0.6 mile to a fork. Turn left at the fork to continue on Beverly Drive. Continue 0.8 mile on Beverly Drive before the road curves to the right onto Franklin Canyon Drive. Drive 1.1 miles to Lake Drive. Turn right on Lake Drive and continue 0.3 miles to the parking area. GPS: N34' 06.679 / W118' 24.901

The Hike

The lower portion of the 600-acre Franklin Canyon Park has a network of trails that winds throughout the shady bottom of the canyon, as well as trails that climb up out of the canyon to viewpoints of the entire canyon, West LA, and on a clear day, even the Pacific Ocean. The Hastain Trail and Discovery Trail can be hiked combined to form a nice loop.

Begin by hiking up the Hastain Trail on the fire road, climbing up the canyon. At just under 1 mile you will come to a viewpoint overlooking a reservoir. This is the lower reservoir, the first one built here before the upper reservoir was added to manage the overflow. Both reservoirs fell into disrepair in 1971 after the Sylmar earthquake and are now used for fishing. They have also been the site of many Hollywood movies and TV show scenes including the famous opening scene from the *Andy Griffith Show*. At this viewpoint there is a wooden trail marker. From here you can continue on up the fire road for another 0.4 mile to get to another viewpoint at the top of the fire road, or for the sake of an easy day hike, make a right turn here off the main trail and begin hiking downhill on the singletrack.

At the bottom of the descent, you will walk through a wide green lawn with an outdoor auditorium all sitting under canopies of sycamore trees. Here you will also see the Doheny House. In 1935 oil baron Edward L. Doheny built a home here in the canyon and used the area as a summer retreat. The adobe house still remains. Cross the large lawn and the road and pick up the start of the Discovery Trail on the other side. The Discovery Trail is a flat easy trail among walnut trees that parallels the road at the bottom of the canyon. At 1.7 miles the Discovery Trail ends at the road. Follow the road back to the start of the Hastain Trail and the parking area.

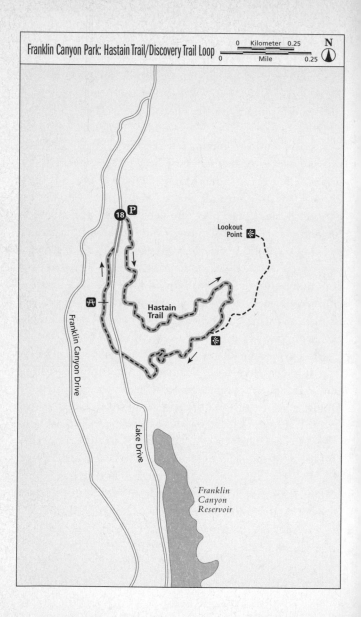

Franklin Canyon Park: Hastain Trail/Discovery Trail Loop

0   Kilometer   0.25

0   Mile   0.25

N

Lookout
Point

18 P

Hastain
Trail

Franklin Canyon Drive

Lake Drive

*Franklin
Canyon
Reservoir*

Miles and Directions

0.0 Begin at the trailhead to the Hastain Trail off Lake Road.

0.2 A small private trail branches off to the right. Continue uphill straight ahead on the fire road.

0.9 Arrive at a lookout spot with a wooden trail marker. If you would like to make the hike longer, continue straight uphill to the peak 0.4 mile ahead. Otherwise, turn right and head downhill on the singletrack trail.

1.3 Arrive at a large grassy lawn. Cross the lawn and the road and pick up the Discovery trailhead on the other side.

1.6 Arrive at a picnic area.

1.7 Arrive back at the road. Continue up the road back to the Hastain trailhead and the parking area.

1.8 Arrive back at the parking area.

Clubs and Trail Groups

Mountains Restoration Trust: This nonprofit land trust preserves land within the Santa Monica Mountains through restoration education and land acquisition. They have regular volunteer events as well as opportunities to hike with, or become, a docent.
3815 Old Topanga Canyon Rd.
Calabasas 91302
(818) 591-1701
www.mountainstrust.org

Sierra Club Angeles Chapter: A grassroots environmental organization that promotes safe and healthy use of the outdoors. Aside from lobbying environmental issues, the Sierra Club leads regular local hikes.
3435 Wilshire Blvd., #320
Los Angeles 90010-1904
(213) 387-4287
Contact.us@angeles.sierraclub.org

Temescal Canyon Association: Originally founded in 1972 to prevent the sale of what is now Temescal Gateway Park, the association helped establish and maintain many trails in the area. They also lead weekly hikes in the summer and monthly hikes in the winter.
P.O. Box 1101
Pacific Palisades 90272
(310) 459-5931
www.temcanyon.org

About the Author

Bryn Fox is a freelance writer living in Carpinteria, California. A graduate of UCLA, Bryn spent four years as an outdoor instructor for UCLA's Outdoor Adventure program, leading students and alumni hiking, rock climbing, and kayaking through the California wilderness. An avid runner, swimmer, and outdoor enthusiast, Bryn now works as a product developer making outdoor gear when she isn't writing or training for her next athletic pursuit.

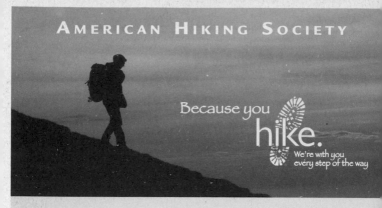

WHAT'S SO SPECIAL ABOUT UNSPOILED, NATURAL PLACES?

Beauty   Solitude   Wildness   Freedom   Quiet   Adventure
Serenity   Inspiration   Wonder   Excitement
Relaxation   Challenge

There's a lot to love about our treasured public lands, and the reasons are different for each of us. Whatever your reasons are, the national **Leave No Trace** education program will help you discover special outdoor places, enjoy them, and preserve them—today and for those who follow. By practicing and passing along these simple principles, you can help protect the special places you love from being loved to death.

THE PRINCIPLES OF **LEAVE NO TRACE**

- Plan ahead and prepare
- Travel and camp on durable surfaces
- Dispose of waste properly
- Leave what you find
- Minimize campfire impacts
- Respect wildlife
- Be considerate of other visitors

Leave No Trace is a national nonprofit organization dedicated to teaching responsible outdoor recreation skills and ethics to everyone who enjoys spending time outdoors.

To learn more or to become a member, please visit us at www.LNT.org or call (800) 332-4100.

Leave No Trace, P.O. Box 997, Boulder, CO 80306